messenger

messenger

poems

R. T. Smith

Louisiana State University Press baton rouge
2001

Designer: Amanda McDonald Scallan
Typeface: Sabon
Printer and binder: Thomson-Shore, Inc.

Library of Congress Cataloging-in-Publication Data:

Smith, R. T.
  Messenger : poems / R.T. Smith.
    p. cm.
  ISBN 0-8071-2674-8 (alk. paper) — ISBN 0-8071-2675-6 (pbk. : alk paper)
  I. Title.
  PS3569.M537914 M47 2001
  811'.54—dc21
00-011289

The author wishes to thank the editors of the following journals, in which some of these poems were previously published, sometimes in different forms: *American Voice*, "Truant"; *Atlantic Monthly*, "Sourwood"; *Atlanta Review*, "Lilting," "Rory"; *Black Warrior Review*, "Linen List"; *Boulevard*, "Spectator"; *Carolina Quarterly*, "Cardinal Directions"; *Connecticut Review*, "His Mirror"; *Cortland Review* (an internet journal), "The Girls of O'Connell Street"; *Crab Orchard Review*, "Orchard," "Road Fever"; *Crazyhorse*, "Pileated"; *Georgia Review*, "Azaleas (1774)," "Fiddle," "North of Spruce Pine," "On House Mountain"; *Gettysburg Review*, "Madeline, *Sotto Voce*"; *Meridian*, "*Ardea Herodias*"; *Partisan Review*, "Bantry Boat"; *Poetry*, "Boy, Recollected," "Horse," "Illumination," "Manicure," "Reading Groups," "Rushlight"; *Poetry Northwest*, "Hardware Sparrows," "Jack-in-the-Pulpit," "Raccoon in the Garden"; *Southern Review*, "Clown," "Coursing," "Twister"; *Sou'wester*, "The Back Road Home"; *TriQuarterly*, "*Au Claire de la Lune*"; *Verse*, "Full Moon with Bells"; *Virginia Quarterly Review*, "Alphabet," "H A N G M A N"; and the Irish journals *Honest Ulsterman*, "Sourwood"; *Irish University Review*, "Illumination," "Linen List"; and *Poetry Ireland Review*, "Lilting."

The author also wishes to thank *Poetry Daily* (www.poetry.com) for featuring several of these poems, Garrison Keillor for reading some of these poems on *Writer's Almanac*, the Virginia Commission for the Arts for grant assistance, and the Dean's Office at Washington and Lee University for travel assistance.

for Sarah

Behold, I show you a mystery:
We shall not all sleep,
But we shall all be changed.

—I Corinthians 15:51

Contents

savor of moss

Sourwood

When the keeper has died,
whose hands have touched
so much honey,

the village will convene
to elect a successor
and to remember

the sweetness of his voice,
his dependable hymns,
the spell of smoke

and the hush just after.
While the elders
resist the old rhythms

of grief, no one will speak
of the ancient belief—
how the beefather's demise,

kept secret, could cause
the death of the hives
in the coming winter.

Then the question will rise
in a nervous murmur:
Who will tell the bees?

On House Mountain

for James Dickey

Here in the grove
of oaks and moonlit mast
I find the scuffed rock

beside a shaking cedar
where last year I saw
the gashed buck bleeding,

his amber eye and savage rack.
He caught my scent,
flicked his white scut

and leaped into the dark.
I can still hear his snort
and the rustle of brush.

I bent down to touch
blood on the dry needles.
Sharp cedar and musk.

I breathed deeply
a night being's hush
rising over and over.

I have come here again
to honor that deer
whose voice I have stolen

for the savor of moss,
for acorns and flowers.
I would speak to the dark

and summon him back,
that moonlit gloss,
in the wind's devoutest hour.

Hardware
Sparrows

Out for a deadbolt, light bulbs
and two-by-fours, I find a flock
of sparrows safe from hawks

and weather under the roof
of Lowe's amazing discount
store. They skitter from the racks

of stockpiled posts and hoses
to a spill of winter birdseed
on the concrete floor. How

they know to forage here,
I can't guess, but the automatic
door is close enough,

and we've had a week
of storms. They are, after all,
ubiquitous, though poor,

their only song an irritating
noise, and yet they soar
to offer, amid hardware, rope

and handyman brochures,
some relief, as if a flurry
of notes from Mozart swirled

from seed to ceiling, entreating
us to set aside our evening
chores and take grace where

we find it, saying it is possible,
even in this month of flood,
blackout and frustration,

to float once more on sheer
survival and the shadowy
bliss we exist to explore.

Jack-in-
the-Pulpit

Herbalists say the taste
is bitter as any sermon.
The root, I mean, or
tuber. The Shrovetide

sermon. And here
in the cul-de-sac where
laurels crowd out sunlight,
I found one stalk opening

its spathe like a cowl
to show the jack in his
white robe narrow
as a warning finger.

All green arc and pious
symmetry without
medicinal use, it seemed
to admonish like Father Mike

hot with the Gospel.
The Epistles, he said,
would scald the tongues
of sinners, and every

impure thought
was a turnpike to hell,
but the lesson was lost
along with the plant's

evangelistic force
when birdsong high
in the cedars psalmed
out, mint-sweet

and oblivious to scripture,
leaving the preacher
looking radish-common
and not likely to do

anyone a whit of good
on either the forest
path or what Saint Gertrude
called the road to rapture.

Raccoon in the Sun Garden

Trimming the redbud whose
splendor was just right
back in April, I gave

the white hollyhocks
a shot at sunlight, as who
would begrudge their

skin-sheer petals access
to radiant July? I have,
after all, a steady good

time meddling in that
garden not of my own
making and never find

more trouble there
than paper wasps or
a black racer, but what

rushed through my rash
mind when I saw
bright eyes amid

the blossoming hosta
was this: what if his
mother (blackberrying

downhill, I guessed)
took offense at my
presence? He gazed

steadily at my face then,
as if to prove himself
no menace, the still

fire of his fur turning mild,
and when I saw him weeks
later by the meadow rill

cleaning a fingerling
rainbow with his forepaws,
he gave me no sign.

Now in raw autumn
the hollyhocks have risen
to resplendence,

and this morning under
the birch turning gold
I found hand prints

with small claws. Evidence
of his scavenger's
existence, though I can't

say if his animation amid
the torn marigolds is kin
to mine or some restless

sign of the season. At night
he gnaws the rake handle
to taste or maybe annihilate

every trace of my salt.

The Back Road Home

Driving Chewacla Road under a sky
of tarnished silver, I took
the curve too fast to brake
for a young buck who had left
his scrape or browsed-out yard
to vault the honeysuckle border
onto the asphalt road like a river.

Magnificent for a moment, almost
frozen in midair, he took
the bumper, headlamp and hood
full in his starboard flank,
spun down broken and stunned,
somehow arose, then hobbled,
scut up and lungs heaving,
into the brush where he lay thrashing.

I parked the bashed car
and followed after, for they cannot
stumble along like us, cannot trust
friends and family to ease them
as they heal. A whitetail, no more
than two winters in the world,
he shuddered and writhed in sharp
weeds of the ember season.

Not even hunters want to see them
suffer, and I will not forget
his eyes looking beyond the cold
moment, past the sweet leaves
and starlit stream. He was stalled
on the thin meridian of pain,
his snapped thighbone trying
still to clear some barrier
wider than dusk or water.

I opened my knife to ease him
over, cradled his jerking muzzle,
then slashed the throat
to free him of all misery
as he struggled for evening air.

Later, driving west again
toward a sky redder than flesh,
I kept my eyes hard on the road,
seeing by the blind headlight
more than before—lustrous fur
poised on every shoulder,
a bone rack radiant
behind every leafless tree.

North of
Spruce Pine

Not a fossil. Rather,
fissures antlered in rock's
sheer wall at roadside.

The small faults jag horns
into the deepest crack
like rivers in a delta

where water meets the sea,
or crown bones a buck
raises from laurel sheen

to catch birth-light, dawn
on a ridge spine. Locked
in the cliff, an image

shimmers through light rain.
I wipe my eyes. What luck
to see myth break to life,

the spiked helmet lifting
with lightning in black
granite. Old thunder is

trembling deep in stone.
At once bright and dark,
a creature wakes, is born

against the literal grain.
Savage that living rock.
Sweet, that morning storm.

Cardinal
Directions

In the body of the cardinal
who hops along the tamarack limbs,
cathedrals are collapsing. Whole
worlds are falling, exhausted
stars and dialects no one left
can translate. This crested finch,
red as the last cannas
wilting, is famished. He scavenges
in a dry season for pods,
cold grubs, any scrap to sharpen
his beak or hone his sight,

and also within me the tree
of bones is giving way
to gravity, the tree of nerves
surrendering, memory's tree
releasing its leaves, though my
eyes are still seeds looking
for fertile soil, and the one bird
heavy in my chest, the cardinal
heart, still has ambitions
to forage, to sing the litany
beyond language, and fly.

Rushlight

What if the year is dying
and the mild and tidy gardener
cherishes under the oak
and loblolly pine both his fire
permit and the pile of stalks
and vines? Angels may be
waking in the nearby swamp
where the laden serviceberry limbs
drag across thick water,

and otters may be following
paths to the bream shallows
where the crust of chalky bear
scat shines under the moon,
in the barren wind, in the shadow
of the drifting tupelo leaf.

Regardless, I will stand in soil
where water and earth arbitrate.
I will see the red hawk dozing
on a bare hemlock limb, see
with the aid of rushlight that rises
from the hollow stems
to make the very air lenticular
and mosslight that hovers as mist
above the browning tendrils
that catch wind or break to settle
in mud and begin the cycle
of legend, that fossil more still
than I am and less in need
of a pastime and less in need
of a burn permit or diminishment

while the rushlight flares
in the calming narrows
and the admonished eye catches fire
and the tall hawk wakes and screams.

Scribe

At the writing table
my sinews tighten,
and a cricket in the sugarbush
is mourning. He is sawing

a cradle and a coffin,
and if he fell forever silent
tonight and went simply rigid
as the soil settled,

green debris rotting
to form a seam of coal
around him, his angles could
be pressed indelibly

into what might resemble
a stone. Someone centuries
from now, if anyone is left,
might unearth a fossil

to find in its insect
outline a symbol and say,
*This is a letter deep
in the alphabet of some ancient*

civilization going where?

Ardea Herodias

The appetite of the blue Heron,
wrote Audubon, is endless,
and I have seen them devour
fish of all kinds, aquatic
insects, young marsh hens
and in captivity even scraps
of cheese and bacon rinds,
but indeed they prefer
fresh swimmers and disdain
to touch anything brought low
by another hunter, although
I have seen one abandon
his cypress nest nearby
the rice fields to contest
a Hawk's catch still animate
in the billhook. The bass
fell to the water and was
lost to both. On another
occasion I shot a male
on the St. John's River
and found in the throat
a fresh perch, its head
severed by the keen
beak. The fish, when
cooked, I found excellent,
but the flesh of an old
Heron itself is by no means
to my taste, not so good
as some epicures would
aver, yet they do devour
occasional seeds, especially
the splendid water lily,
which sweetens the sinews.
I myself should prefer
the meat of a young Eagle—
which it shames me to kill,

though I too am a carnivore—
or even that beacon of sorrow
by which prophets once swore,
the omnivorous scavenger
and sarcast of the willows,
your commonest black Crow.

Audubon's
Cardinal

The ailing artist shivers
in Vieux Carré and pulls
his Seminole jacket tighter,
then leans across to catch
the imagined flicker of eye.
The bird on paper stiffens,
as if the silhouette first
sketched on an elm stump,
then the etchings, even
the meticulous paints he
now thickens, won't mend
the muslin breast where lead
pellets struck. He tells
himself it's not guilt
that prevents the miracle.
Heron, bittern, junco and
vulture—he's killed them
by the hundreds, but always
with one ambition, to catch
a song in three dimensions—
insinuation, color, line.
Audubon lifts the bone cup
of chicory to his lips,
then turns again. He wants
the cardinal alive, a stalled
forager perched curious
on a hickory limb in autumn,
the music restored, but
all he gets is effigy,
the prophet's mirror, gall.
The eye, despite his vigor
and precision, shines like
glass, the red wing brittle
as ice. His most expensive
brushes, pigments shipped
from France, the artist's
articulate sight—they all

add up to taxidermy, and not
the blasphemy he's after.
He almost laughs to recall
the day he roosted high
on a sweetgum limb to watch
a brace feeding, the female
quick and oblivious over
a scatter of seeds, her mate
in the blue spruce, his
brassy *chak,* the dry pitch
of a musket's cocking.
He alone remembers. Hours
by oil lamp, sunlight, dusk,
he has labored to render
feathers and crest lifelike,
the mask, the amber claws.
Primaries litter the table.
Small blades. A convex lens.
The original skull yellows
on the sill, and Audubon is
spellbound by his failure
to overcome death with
artifice and sheer will.
No breath, no resurrection,
and the artist coughs, rises
to wipe bristles and his
bloody spittle on a rag,
then turns to his journal
and scratches with a goose
quill in sinuous cursive
that is almost flight itself:
cul-de-sac, this work is
madness, yet I'll try again.
The last candle blown, sleet
spatters the pane like so
many wild beaks pecking.
At last, to pursue a darker

secret, he lifts his silver
flute from a Persian shawl,
and scarlet music flows
as through a hollow bone,
improvisations against rigor,
cardinal cantatas till dawn.

Azaleas (1774)

The red ones, ephemeral, festive in time
for early Easter—"Swamp honeysuckle"

Bartram called them, and sketched quickly,
knowing they were close to rhododendrons

he'd found in windbreak coves
where the Appalachian chain shadowed any

thought of spring. Also cousin to highland heather,
and he recalled their name behind the fragrant

momentary blossoms was from the classical
Greek for "dry." Even as he saw them

across the Savannah River's soiled waters
as bursts of wildfire inexplicable

in the time of green, he studied the seed
vessels, tasted the root and was sure

the fast sap could not long prevent
such loose panicles of flowers from withering.

The branches' white hardwood opened
to his knife. He found the scent bitter.

Nothing like this existed in all of Europe's
dark forests or tyrannical gardens, but

he was not homesick, he told his journal,
not Ovid in exile, though all about him

the landscape changed and clouds shifted
so quickly he thought it could only be

the work of a god. Vagrant on this savage
landscape, he did not wish to dwell

in nostalgia for the Passion, the Host
cool upon his tongue or cathedral

echoes, and yet, out there in the Territories,
April looming, shagbark and tulip trees

loosening pollen, sassafras rampant, he found
science inadequate and settled

by the fatwood fire to read Luke's gospel
aloud. Even mapping his daily transit—

the congress of flood-rich rivers, pinewoods,
azalea-strewn slopes still magical

long after sunset—he could discern only
the Lamb pierced and broken, His suffering

never softened by Latin catalogues
of genus and species. The spread petals,

sudden outcrops of untamed color, his own
fibers tightening—it all taught a single lesson,

the question of estrangement. Secular
in every bone the year before, he had dreamed

of drawing bud and leaf-sheen with a birch
pencil. Now, even asleep, he prayed

for dawn and a sense of mission,
the wilderness a miracle he was meant to list

like Adam, the Adam of plants, though this
was far from Eden and the Swede Linnaeus

had set the precedents. He wished
for subtle pigments to set the heat of azaleas

exact in his ledgers, and that was the first
week out, reconnoitering before the straggling

retinue caught up, before fever,
moccasins, hard crossings and the bewildered

circling. He discovered also four species of biting
flies and a glittering rivulet rising

wild and brilliant from the shadow
of a skull-shaped stone. He could almost

discern the form of Eve dazzling amid sunshafts.
He wrote between calfskin covers, "In a paradise

fallen, I am westbound, stunned by the benison
of azaleas and celebrating Zion alone."

Madeline,
Sotto Voce

A whole family of hothouse
flowers, we Ushers suffered
apathy, thin skin of a poppy,
the same strange eyes as any
doomed species. Aristocrats,
we cloistered for safety, all
silver, velvet cloth and crystal,
but I was not that simple.
I craved to escape the smother
of sibling love. I said, "Give
me air." My blood ran thinner.
My brother swore of sounds
so faint not a mouse could
hear, the weight of soothing
light. I swooned in that unholy
atmosphere. *The lady
Madeline was no more.*
Roderick locked me in the crypt.
I dreamed and shivered as he
sulked and fiddled. Did he
remember loving to touch
translucent skin across my
wrist, my gossamer hair?
Oh, he refused any real tryst,
but his stifled desire summoned
a gothic storm. Now our
story's every listener asks
how I could sibyl out
at the exquisite moment
of fracture and collapse.
This much I can say:
a woman will remember
how her pins and brooches
have edges. A woman will
whittle away at death's ebony
to sing her morning song.

I swore to reach the light
and wed my shrouded whisper
to a twin's riven terror.
I conjured the mighty
voice of a thousand waters,
to annihilate all narrative
in the sheer and bitter air.

human salt

Alphabet

In the sewing room
the mail-order Singer
with its chrome-rimmed
wheel and gleaming needle
was turned under
to make a desk while
mother started dinner.

I faced west where
the window shimmered.
For an hour I rehearsed
my letters, spelling
everything visible—
zipper and scissors,
thimbles and spools.
The oval mirror made
the wallpaper zinnias
flower still further,
and a mantel clock
held the minutes back.

The Eagle pencil
in my cramped hand
scratched fishhook
j or an *l* like a needle.
Late sunlight glazed
the holly leaves silver
beyond the peeling sill.
While I squinted hard
at the Blue Horse paper,
the twilight world
held perfectly still.

When I was finished,
each curve and flourish
set in disciplined rows,

fresh tea with ice
appeared at my elbow,
the yellow *c* of lemon
in the tumbler's perfect *o,*
and if mother had praise
for what I had done,
I would shine all evening
bright as a straight pin,
while the new moon
with its careless serifs
cleared the trees and rose.

Reading Groups

Five blackbirds sat in the corner circle,
slow with books, Miss Noonan claimed.
Cardinals and Robins crooned
the antics of Dick and prissy Jane
for extra milk and tinfoil stars
while my flock struggled. We read
aloud or doodled. I preferred
Genesis, Grit, The Atlanta Constitution
("Covers Dixie Like the Dew"),
reports of train wrecks,
Lester Maddox, Tech football
and barbecues. *Stop that cloud
gathering,* her stern voice said.
Her plastic ruler slapped my hand,
but I was elsewhere, wind-borne, flying.
The welt across my palm burned red
as the rose on a blackbird's wing.

Messenger

We shall not all sleep,
but we shall all be changed.

Two nights he came to me, mute,
on fire, no dream. I woke to find
the window embered and fog filling
the willows. The third time
he was milder and early, his gray form
all ash. He said to me at bedside, kneeling,
"You must say your life to save it."
Midnight, hoarfrost. I was not yet ten
and didn't know what to make of so brief
a bedtime story. His features
were simple and familiar—the smile,
both eyes shut in bliss, I guessed,
head and torso echoing an antique
keyhole. From sleep's icy edge
I asked, "How?" But he was gone,
the room all hazed. The air smelled
of struck matches, scuppernong,
a copperhead's musk. What next?
The moon was new in the budding
bird cherry and Venus startling overhead.
Dizzy for water, I followed
my flashlight down the stairs
where the black mantel clock
was bonging. Beside it sat the twin
of my herald, a stone bookend
from Kildare and no more able
to speak or take wing than a weathercock.
His closed eyes told me, "Look
inside," but I ached to see him blaze
again and say aloud how change
could shake me to a shining. "But
I must be the key," I thought,
and stepped over the sparkling threshold.
My nightshirt floated ghostly

across the scalded lawn, under the arbor,
beside the barn, my soles not troubled
by white grass crackling
all the way to the well shed,
the burning that must
have been coming from me.

Horse

Tired of writing at the desk
my father refinished over Christmas,
I stared into the walnut-stained
maple with flaws in the grain

floating like clouds, and then
some mischief made me draw,
in that room away from fields
I'd grown to love, the outline

of a horse, my best to date.
I was twelve. Still worse,
impressed with my work, I decided
to carve those curves into the wood.

Inch by inch with a Barlow
knife, I made the figure
stand there forever, every year
more inaccurate and absurd,

though still in motion, still sleek.
And sometimes now, if I hurry
to write, the pen racing breakneck
will slip over the small furrow

and into the flank, raised forelock
or the face of a horse
that still stumbles across
Connemara heather to mark

a desire old as cave painting,
the wish to entice some wild thing
and make beauty local,
to bring something graceful

close to the language of home.

Fiddle

Locked tight in blue
velvet as a fossil
saved in slate,

the fiddle my father
played in church,
on the courting porch

and for the Masons
of Griffin, Georgia,
is covered in dust.

Bridge missing, scrollwork
chipped and pegs
spoiled with chrome,

it harbors a secret
in its sound box:
Carlo Bergonzi,

fece in Cremona,
1733. An authentic
antique made

from bird's-eye
maple, fir, the glue
and varnish kin

to Guarneri and Strads,
it is, he says,
our single treasure.

The bow, now
missing, was tipped
with amber and fine

as heron bone.
The strings are
raveled to floss.

And yet, he lifts
the hourglass shape,
snugs the chin rest

and pretends to serenade
mother with ghostly
tones, his wrist

deftly turning, fingertips
gripping a shadow,
as rosin scent

somehow sweetens
the kitchen air.
Is it "Raglan Road"

that animates mother
or "Shady Grove"?
"The Kerry Trance"?

When she stops wiping
dishes to begin
her bashful shuffle,

I start to sway myself
and savor the legacy
they offer—illusory

tunes, a past relived
with vigor, a vintage
Italian fiddle that kept

their story musical
until the marriage
melody became

their lasting dance.

Boy, Recollected

Grandmother in the summer kitchen's
lean-to breeze said, "Towhead,
your cowlick sticks out like a wing,"
and off I sped to the meadow
where a brown bossy ran her tongue
over Johnson grass after the saline
tang. "Wings," I echoed, "wings."
I saw the pattern of shaped
blades tousled as my hair but green
and ran on toward the bough-house
beside the minnow stream, wind licking
across my brow and sweaty shock,
like some mischievous browser after
that child-sweet and human salt.

Manicure

Coral nails on white formica,
Mother tapped to Patsy Cline.
The Motorola's golden speaker
wailed. I'd hide my soldiers
with bazookas in the oven.
Iced tea, pot roast, turnip greens
and yams. The wall clock kept
the beat. The daffodils wilted,
mother flicked her Jesus fan,
with Boo in the playpen,
laughing. Filter cigarette,
dash of Gilbey's gin, faintest
whisper of My Sin. Father
working overtime. The clean
plate at the end of the table
shone bright as any shrine.

His Mirror

A room of blue dahlias,
the deathbed and cedar chest,
an oak chifforobe with full-length
glass on the door, but he was
gone to earth and angels, his
khaki work shirts, crimped slouch
hat and tool belt idle. I stood
and worried the keyhole,
but my knife and wire never fit.
In the months after, the room
growing dust, I saw the mirror
losing silver along the edges.
The dark back-coat was moss
spreading on ice or weather-smut
taking over an old headstone.
I worried when the silver was
all gone the door would open
to cracked knotwood staring back
and empty hangers jangling,
that I would no longer be able
to say I had his eyes.

Under the Orchard

Aunt Moira's quick knife cut
the sunset to chips, peels limp as skin
and an angry seed in every center.
"We came over," she lisped,
"on Oglethorpe's ships, a gaggle
of bogside debtors spat out
to empty the London prisons.
O'Connor sowed a hundred rows
of clingstone pits and prayed
for an easy winter. Two centuries
of sweat brought us peace at last."
White ice cream slush in the bowl
made a full moon. The churn
on its tarnished axis turned.
We spooned the sweet dessert,
then deep under a Sunday evening
sky blue as Holy Mary's veil
I skipped across the lawn
singing, "We were the jailbirds,"
my eyes alert for English sons,
peach bits bright as fireflies
still succulent on my tongue.

Sorceress

Granny Johnson swore a cock cardinal
was the devil's angel, his red
the tea rose color of my heart. She kept
wing feathers wrapped like a sachet
in her bedside drawer. Sen-sen on her
breath, she swore to reveal my future,
call up any secret from my soul.
Sleepwalking with her silver hair
trailing, she held a heavy candle
no one awake could see. I hid
behind the black piano. Window open,
she spoke to stars, said my Christian
name's Pig Latin. I heard birdcalls
across the meadow, told God I would
always, I would never. The clamor
of wings. I saw the curtains breathe.

Twister

Season shifting, our pond
taut as a drum, the meadow
was heavy with crows. Every leaf
was still. A stripe of green
horizon tinted the evening,
and then it came, a swirl
of bats, a column of smoke,
the black angel playing
his hosannahs, his dervish
wind like the Wednesday freight.
The firehouse siren grieved,
and we nestled in the cellar
amid last year's apples,
protruding roots and gallons
of jam. Nervous as spiders
when Isaiah said their names,
we listened to chaos scouring
the earth and prayed
for the angel to leave us
admonished but unmaimed.

Truant

One Sunday I skipped the lesson
to walk behind the crosses
and mossy slabs. I saw
where the doe had fallen
the winter before, her thawed body
gone to bone and carrion,
and over her a shimmer
provisional as the music of flutes,
as if sunlight . . . as if resurrection. . . .
Edging closer, I saw it was
a multitude of sulphurs
feasting near the holy ground.
Later, kneeling at the rail,
I raised my eyes
to the Virgin's likeness,
and saw again that levitation,
that golden shawl.

C l o w n

Fevered, itch-mad, splotched from ear
to toe, I heard the doctor solemn
as a judge say, *chicken pox*. I felt
feathers in my throat and thought even
morning math class must be better.
No tumbler of iced ginger ale or
Sergeant Rock comics could ease
the torture. On the radio, Gene Autry
yodeled. The sky beyond the window
was willow-ware blue. Waxed fruit
weighted the bureau down. Saint cards
lining the mantel like a circus almost
glowed. I could hear ants in the grass,
buds of the crepe myrtle as they opened.
Half asleep, I dreamed I wore tattoos
of a savage race. The pictures moved.
Then mother came in with cloth
on a bolt. As I napped, she snipped
and stitched till a clown suit stepped
out, white cotton covered in scarlet
spots. *Now you can be Berries
the Clown*, she said. These were
the vestments my suffering had earned.
Her voice filled the room with laughter.
High in the conifers a cardinal burned.

Revival

When sap ambered the scarred apple branch,
I skipped church to play Scrabble on the porch.
On my knees with seven letters

I acted Adam, eager to order the world.
The first word rooted in the board's
central star. In an hour I had a crossword

garden that nearly made sense of birdcall,
rose of Sharon, a balmy morning.
When an engine droning down the road

became a dark flurry circling, then bent
a sapling's limb, I was afraid.
It was bees, six million tempers shaping

a pendant's glitter around a banished queen.
I tried to spell them into oblivion,
to tame *manic* to *man* and transform

ape to *rapture*. I wanted shelter from a storm
more zealous than any sermon.
But then I saw their frenzy for pollen.

In quest of summer balm, they cast
a sunlit glamour. Too busy
and spellbound for stinging,

the colony was offering me their psalm,
first time ever I had been ready
to hear their rhapsody,

to see them rise and swarm.

H A N G M A N

Harpers Ferry

High on a roofer's scaffold
I connect the far dots of Orion,
The Great Bear and The Swan,
but I also invent The Gallows

from a dozen scattered stars
and see Osawatomie climbing
the thirteen steps to heaven,
as Miss Isley's hand appears,

sketching a gibbet, scrawling
white chalk on slate, trapdoor
dashes for the secret word.
Just after lunch, we had to guess

the letters. With each mistake
she'd add a limb as the stickman
we called Old John Brown
swung into view. Whoever solved

the puzzle got to dust erasers,
instead of feigning a nap.
A skinny kid with questions
and first in my class to mess

with codes and tangles, I was
the last chosen for softball
or folk dancing on rainy days.
Eager to hear my name

called out, I knew how it felt
to be strangling, but at hangman
I was quickest. "An *l*," I'd say,
"a *t*. The word's *assault!*"

Again tonight, I imagine Brown
outlined in white, a riddle who
believed in taking truth by storm.
In fact, clouds muster

to the west, and thunder
seems to ask if I would dance
on air to know the answer:
how can a grown man

be saved by games? The world
is less stable than a scaffold.
Then the first spatter of rain
dispels the constellations.

No stars, no names but blurry
night, and I am sentenced again
to earth. I come down counting
my blessings, bone by weary bone.

spectator

Illumination

As if some monk bored
in the cold scriptorium
had let his quill

wander from the morning
Gospel, two tendrils
of wisteria

have scrolled
their green fervor
into the weave of a wicker

deck chair to whisper
with each spiral,
every sweet leaf

and dew sparkle,
Brother, come
with us, come home.

Lilting

Donegal

In the lull just after
McKenna's reel, a girl
with a port-wine

stain upon her
throat stood delicate
as a heron, while

the hard-faced farmers
all froze. Head tilted
and both eyes closed,

she soared two octaves
and trilled as a local
grocer hummed

the drone. The surf
and bramble of Irish
syllables filled

the pub between
sill and lintel,
sweeter than linnets,

more urgent than
a crow. And the scent
of raw lavender

was anchored in it,
thrifty and radiant
as a mouse's clean

bones. Not even
the barman dared
clink a glass,

and every villager
listened, as her
wordless notes

shivered, then rose.
A century ago
on winter nights

like this, to the tune
of no instrument
but such a supple

tongue, two dozen
outlaw couples
in a shuddered

room whirled
and shuffled
to defy the priests

who banned the flutes
and smashed every
fiddle on a stone.

Within the hushed
moment before chat
and porter could

once again flow,
she held every eye
with the weary glow

of a wilting lily,
and the wind outside
was talking treason,

quiet as woodbine
embroidering a trellis
or native moss

softening the nest
of a heron
just after she's flown.

Linen List

Annaghmakerrig

The mulberry ink
of some matron's perfect
cursive has dried the color
of rust, and by firelight

the ordinary words are
illuminated to scripture:
dishing cloths and common
towels, frilled pillow cases

and twilled sheets.
In the adjacent chamber
Irish girls filled the hot
press daily and whispered

about the ostler in his
livery or delicate ladies
whose oil portraits glow
in the halls. From Cootehill

and Newbliss, Monaghan
proper and the parish called
Agabog they came, a flock
of poor girls with skin

like cream in the cat's
dish. No ballad or sketch
preserves their names
or faces in this house

called "Rock of the River"
in awkward Irish. Surrounded
by cows, a bog and dirty
weather, they kept every

fish napkin and doily

creased and clean
for the houseproud Powers,
who wanted each milk bottle

counted and the larder
locked. Aisling, Cliona
and half-lame Siobhan—
they lived on brown

bread and filched apples;
they suffered burns
from the flatirons
and the linen mistress'

tongue. "Mice of the house,"
she called them, and kept
each girl on the run,
though they giggled behind

their fists on Sunday,
walking to mass along
the rhododendron path.
But in the attic, one

might wake in her narrow
berth to whisper
the sorrowful Mysteries
and ask Heaven's Blue Mary

to send her a ruddy
farmer before dawn brought
the distant hillside twilled
green with close-grown

firs and the routine
checking of chapter

and verse from the linen
list. Then the scolding,

treks to the back-kitchen,
a life of skittering about
and "yes, mum," spoken
across the turf stove's

inferno or a billow
of steam by the rocks
of this weary river,
the pillars of this dream.

Bantry Boat

Turf craft, they call it, a slab pressed flat
and stamped by Wild Goose Studio in Cork
with the Bantry Boat, St. Brendan and four
monks afloat on a sea of crosses, their currach

a new moon, a rib, a ripe slice of melon.
I hiked someone's pasture in a sun shower
to view the gray pillar my guidebook touted
as the legendary Kilnaurane stone.

The evening bay shone chalice silver.
North wind waved a sea across the meadow,
along Rope Walk Road and the swinging gate.
Four oarsmen and their stern navigator

were almost rubbed smooth by tourists, weather,
the itchy sheep. I could just make them out,
their scythe of a boat vertical, its prow
facing heaven and the rain. What I have now

is this palm-sized replica where stout
sailors are straining, their faces eager.
Someone's brainchild, this new use for peat
from the duty-free makes a cheap souvenir,

green as a tortoise box washed in shadows.
It's always cool as moss in that sun shower
I wish to remember, the fleecy meadow,
my need to see the remnant plinth, mythic

enterprise, pilgrimage of sheer spirit.
The relic of brothers rowing a dreamboat
now harbors on the brim of my kitchen sink,
where it should be kept, before the window,

trim and ready, exposed to moonlight,
forever handy, and close to moving water.

Au Claire de la Lune

for Geroid Ó Cathain

In the gray Fifties—the wake
of the Great War, the shortage—
the last child on the Blasket—
no playmate but conies
and a calf, no sport or rival
but the graceful gulls—
was told the tallow ration
was too meager for reading
or keeping at bay the dark.

At his studies by day he found
an old story in the Irish tongue,
how the island fishermen
filled a shell with mackerel oil
and ran a rush through it
to wick the spark.
Sprawled across his pallet
with books and a tablet,
he learned the work of French,
maths, Scheherazade
by the mollusk lamp's light.

His science page called
the shell an *atremis.*
A shy creature lived inside,
alert for the moon's *open sesame.*
It followed the tides and kept
his secret. Under the spell
of its midnight flicker
the boy grew fluent, his ear
keen, eyes astute as a lark's.

When at last the door opened
and the island was abandoned,
he sang the song he'd learned—
*je n'ai plus de feu . . . pour
l'amor de Dieu*—and crossed

the salt water to the world's
green feast—ink-smudged,
fish-smelling, Aladdin's lamp
shut snug in his valise.

Full Moon
with Bells

As the solstice moon
with its Latin landscape
rises waferlike
above the quay,

moonlight and frost
embroider the slate
with a guidebook
Irish beauty, and I shut

off the radio's report
of your sad story—
rape by a neighbor,
the court forbidding

a foreign abortion,
the power of Rome.
Where is mercy?
The boats are in,

the city still, the priory's
new bells summoning
all of Galway to vespers.
Now I imagine you

moongazing through lace
curtains as the tides
of your body ossify,
the first blue milk

forming intricate
as snowflakes high
in the winter air.
I want to reassure you,

but the words fail me,

and neither sweet
litany nor the Host
glowing can show me

anything holy
in the bishop's decree.
The faraway moon's
ancient names I whisper—

Mare Serenitatus
and *Lacus Somniorum*—
offer no solace,
while worshipers approach

the altar, their eyes
too filled with piety
to see. In Dublin
the state ministers

caucus over blue cigar
smoke and brandy,
but no absolution
echoes in the bronze

of those vernacular
bells, as the country
ices over, *Patria
Incognita,* cold core

of the heart, dark face
of the moon.

Pileated

Twilight, the Irish hour,
and a woodpecker drums
on the fungal hickory stump.
He could be after sleeping grubs
or summoning a publican.
Warmed by the fire of his own
red crest, he is ready to down
a pint, to talk a little treason
and listen to the evening music.
His eye in the dying light is
gleaming. I want to take him aside
like some Sligo republican
and ask what hope he holds for truce
and if he can keep the covenant,
but he interrupts his hammering
and stands stiff as a Roman
stamped on a coin. Is it just
intimation of the cold front coming
that arrests him in mid-rhythm,
or the glare from my spyglass
caught in the dying light?
His expression under that red
cap is all sinister wisdom,
as he struts about the stump,
strikes a pose, then spreads
his wings, as if summoned
on some covert mission.
Immune to any surveillance,
he enters the menacing dark.

The Girls of O'Connell Street

for Brendan Galvin

The brash klaxon of a Guinness lorry
shivers the air where the cashiers
and salesgirls of Dublin steer
swift as a regatta past
the Liberator's lofty effigy
and the mossgreen
bronze statue of Joyce.
Sloop-elegant and subdued
by formula fashion,
except when the sun
catches an earring
blazing like a Viking blade,

they glide and tack in twilled
wool and linen, amazing
for their deft navigation
through frenzy, all trim
rigging, the grace of necessity
and obligatory smiles.
Ready to clock in,
sort change and set the kettle,
they lend the morning a symmetry
almost puritan, routine wed to duty,
all dreams tightly leashed,

until one imp from the country
with gold in her nose
and magenta dreadlocks appears
from absolutely nowhere,
narrow keel to the wind
and rainbow shawls flying,
her laughter swiftly unstitching
any edict of taste or election
ever decreed by Calvin
Klein, or even Calvin.

Road Fever

Before I was born the evicted
Irish walked this road,
with no notion where to aim
their anger. What was left

of their households bruised
their shoulders. What remained
was a broken gate and the reek
of spoiled potatoes.

They boiled tack leather.
They sipped rain from ivy.
Beyond a ditch where the weary
sought shelter, in pennyroyal

and weeds I discover
the memorial cut to a boundary
stone: *1848/Sorrow/Our Mother.*
Typhus struck them—sister, child,

farmer—lice-borne, or carried
by touch. The word in Greek
means *mist,* like the brothy
fog bewitching the evening

air. What I have read
is this: their brows burned
and skin speckled like buckshot
as they fell. I should stop

everything to kiss the ground
that a roof in nearby Kilmurry
waits for me, that the downy
fringe of blight no longer

infests the food.
I should push my hand
wrist-deep into the healthy
earth and press my ear

to the road for its story:
they walked here, they wept,
they haunt the wind.
But the night will be soft,

and I will find a stuffed fox
in the parlor, and lavender.
A girl will bring me a dash
of whisky against the sleet

chill. A table will be set
before me with oat farls
and berry jam as faces
from Gort or Ennis flower

in kettle steam and tenant
the starless evening air.

In Jest

for Andrew Hudgins

Man walks down a Belfast alley;
it's night—you've heard the story,
it has to be a story—and a voice
from the dark presses a muzzle
to his temple: "Catholic or Protestant?"
That's the question, posed in a roguish
rhythm, and the tourist, fool,
daredevil, whatever, protests, "I'm
a Buddhist," but the voice insists:
"Are you a Catholic Buddhist or
a Protestant Buddhist?" End of story.
Or end of the joke, but there's blood
staining the cinders in the morning.

One party sends a car full of Semtex
for fireworks and random carnage.
The others visit a pub with guns
and black bandannas. We learn to pray:
Our Father who art indifferent, shadows
be thy name, blown to kingdom
come, give us our daily . . . thy bloody
will be done. "Why is it the sun
never set on the British Empire?"
"God wouldn't trust the buggers
in the dark." This is the cadence
of deadly jest, smothering with shame
all music of harbor and hearth.
And what is left of ancestral glory,
rhythms of anvil, oar and harp,
the story beyond the end of the story
in the country of the riven heart?

Rory

Before I was anywhere the fox
crept into the henyard. It was
lovely. He was brighter than rust
and russet. The stalking moon
was his ally. The fence
was useless. He was sleek fire
by the pump, in the ivy, smiling
under the fig tree. Among fifty
chickens he was ruthless, lost
in bloodthirst. Amid the last
fireflies and the dwindling
chivaree of black crickets,
he brushed the bird cherry's
scarred trunk and vanished.

How mother knew for certain
she was with child was simple—
a scattered litter of feathers,
the air altered with elegant
stealth. Cold mud flowers
of his paw prints led hunters
into the woods past the willow.

Over the door going down
to the root cellar a carved fox
was leaping in the stone lintel.
When I was an infant, mother
lifted me and raised my rosy
hand to stroke the muzzle.
Cobwebs lay across the grass
like smoke billows. Autumn,
and the woods were scorched
with secrets. The thistles
stirred. How do you know
what you will be? Something
moves through the mist of sleep

to touch you. Something quick
and luminous brings a name
for your hunger and the reek
of need the world calls *musk*.
It offers you a voice
infused with cunning flame.

Coursing

Collegiate Church of St. Nicholas, Galway

Again, the Spanish Arch,
then Lynch's
window of the pitiful son,
until a chill rain

pelts me to the church
with an inner door
whose limestone reach
is carved with a cur

hackling the sinister niche,
a coney on the opposite,
two points of a torc.
The brochure explains:

the hound of Heaven
(all leap and muzzle)
pursues the hare
of the Soul (so much

crouching tremble).
It goes on forever.
As I stretch
my hand to touch

eroding stone
chiseled to fur,
a hidden switch
is thrown, and floodlights

blaze like a hundred
torches. The portal
and porch are lit
as if to catch

and dazzle me,

after ten visits, still
hard on the search,
the heat of the hunt,

until I find myself—
half dog, half rabbit—
once again seeking
in this ancient church

the face of the spirit
and haven from the rain.

At Luggala

Up from Dublin on the run
from a cold bed
and a bad marriage,

I came to the cobbler's
cottage, misty glens
and a lake. I had

Wicklow honey and Chinese
tea for comfort, foxgloves
and yellow gorse fields

bleating with sheep.
The first evening splitting
chips from Irish oak

like iron, I found
in a limb's center, which
some call the heart,

strands of russet hair
locked in the wood's
ancient grain.

After apples and bread,
I studied the tresses,
then pleated a red bracelet

that eased me to sleep.
Wind lashed the window
with rain. In a twist

of sheets I woke
from dream—Daphne's
flight from the god.

He was all light
and order. She was
a river's wild daughter.

She screamed, heart
riven, and entered
the tree, leaving only

her anger, but there
in the room shadows
flared. In firelight

the knotty pine was all
eyes. Across heather,
falling water and stone

a woman's voice rose,
or was it the curlew's
morning cry? The quoit

of hair wound tight
on my wrist. The trees
were leaning. Was it

fever that shaped my
wife's face in the glass,
drowning in sorrow,

rooted in flame?
Or perhaps regret
for the death of remorse,

the shiver of failure
glazing the split
timbers with shame?

Spectator

In "The Dead" when the whole
Epiphany party agrees
that some monks sleep in their coffins
to remind them of mortality
and do penance for our sins,

we all know the revelers are wrong,
embellishing hearsay, inviting
medieval rumors into dying
Ireland, but by the time Mrs.
Malins insists the monks are

holy men, I've already become
half Trappist, my Gabriel
regrets lost in the story under
Michael Furey. I'm wishing
myself south to Mount

Melleray, anticipating sanctuary,
the safety of matins and lauds,
long hours of Good Works
and Latria. I want to be free
as the pious brothers are free

of quarreling over the wishbone,
of blowing my own horn
till the ones I love suffer and fall.
Alone with a worn book, I want
to be scourged and shriven,

to lie still in the long house
of my coffin, while outside,
snow falls on the crooked crosses.
But then the sweets and sherry
are served, hostesses beaming,

Gabriel fortified for his annual
address, and I am back at the table,
a veteran spectator knowing
how false he'll ring and already
thirsty for Gretta's big scene

after "The Lass of Aughrim." I am
blind again to candles
in the monastic chapel. I'm deaf
to glad Latin and still,
in spite of the beauty

of Joyce's cold story,
self-tortured beyond the snow's
tenebrous *Ego te absolvo,*
spoken softly to the world.